Title: Stop Fading Away!

By Cathy Shuter

Subtitle: Learn how to receive t... deserve.

Introduction:

Is this book for you?

Complete this quiz to find out:

1. Are you the kind of person who spends their time worrying about other people, hoping they are O.K. and doing what you can to help them? Yes/No

2. Do you try and help friends and family whenever you can? Yes/No

3 Do you have a caring job? (Teacher, Nurse, Carer, Doctor etc.) Yes/No

4. Do you love helping others but end up leaving yourself with little time and energy to look after yourself? Yes/No

5. Do you secretly wish that other people would notice how much you do, how busy you are and offer to help you sometimes? Yes/No

6. Do you feel worn out and even a bit resentful? Yes/No

7. Do you feel guilty when you put yourself first? Yes/No

Award yourself a point for every 'Yes.'

Did you score 4 points or more?

Yes?

Then you need to read this book!

Introduction: Why Are So Many Of Us Fading?

Life has its challenges. We try our best to be good people and to get by. We do the things we need to do in order to survive, and many of us are feeling worn out.

I believe that the vast majority of people would score 4 or more points in the quiz, as humans are generally loving and caring. They want to help. The trouble is, we humans can find it hard to express our own needs and feelings, even to ourselves.

Life has suddenly got tougher for many. Even people who were happily jogging along with life are starting to struggle.

As I write this, it is Summer 2022. So much has happened and I am taking some time to reflect on my own life as well as what is happening more generally in the world.

I have been thinking about life from all sorts of different perspectives.

We are all so busy.

We have so many things to get done and there appear to be increasing obstacles to thwart our efforts. It can be draining. Quite a few of us suspect that we are in real danger of fading.

What do I mean by fading exactly?

Think of things that fade. I am imagining a bright blue tee-shirt. It is beautiful and vibrant. It attracts attention. Over time, and many washes, the vivid colour starts to fade. The tee-shirt is still functional, you can wear it if you want to, but by now, the colour has faded to a murky grey. At this point, it is also stretched out of shape and may even have a few holes in. Most people cast a tee-shirt like this aside and buy a bright new one.

Humans can feel washed out and cast aside in the same way. They feel drained and they worry that they aren't as appealing or interesting as they used to be. As a result of this feeling, they may start to withdraw from life.

Some people may stop going out and spending time with others, convincing themselves that no one would miss them if they didn't bother turning up. They might stop doing the things they used to enjoy because they believe that they only have enough time and energy to carry out the basics of life such as earning a living and feeding themselves.

At this point people may crave a return to happier, more sociable times, but they notice that their associates haven't put up much of a fight on their behalf, friends don't seem that bothered that they don't turn up anymore. Feeling rejected like this, can lead to feelings of hopelessness.

Have you been feeling like this?

The trouble is, that other people cannot read your mind. They don't know how you are feeling unless you tell them. If you stop meeting up with them without explaining why, they may assume that you are avoiding them by choice and eventually they will stop asking to meet up with you. They may do this believing that this is what you really want.

When I think of all the people that I suspect are feeling increasingly lonely and cut off from others, I want to find a solution. I ask myself, what is the remedy?

I have been pondering this for a while now and have read as much as I can on the subject. I have concluded that we tend to look for external solutions to help us feel better. We tell ourselves that if we 'buy that car' or 'go on that holiday', things will feel better. Sometimes we do feel happier for a while, but often we return to our faded state, more tired and worn out than before.

Until we realise that we must begin with ourselves, we are likely to end up in a cycle of fading, then looking for external solutions, feeling a little better before fading again.

This book has been written to support you in your efforts to feel brighter and more balanced.

The approaches discussed are likely to help many people, but if you are in any doubt consult an appropriate professional before proceeding.

We are all different and what works for one person may be less effective for another.

Chapter 1: Surviving.

Fading can affect any of us. It doesn't matter about our age or gender. Let's briefly explore what we all need in order to feel OK.

A baby literally won't survive long if their basic needs aren't attended to. They must have sleep, to be fed and changed. They require so much more than this though. They need to be cuddled and loved. If babies don't get cuddles and love, they start to suffer emotionally. This can have far-reaching consequences even in their adult lives.

From an early age, babies become aware of the give and take of communication. They cry and they are fed. As they get older, they mimic the sounds made to them by their care givers and are rewarded with smiles and praise. This is how they learn to talk.

A toddler needs basic care, cuddles, and love too. They are also eager to explore their world safely and learn new skills. If they miss out on this, they suffer.

A young child in school may have all the love, nurture, and care available to them at home but in school they also need to feel cared for and valued by staff and pupils. Friendships become very important at this stage, so if a child does not feel they have friends, they are likely to fade. If staff fail to appreciate their unique skills, children are likely to feel inadequate. They may consider that they don't compare well with the other pupils.

Teenagers need to feel cared about by their families. They want to feel welcome and valued at school, and at this age, their peers are so very important to them. If they feel rejected by their peers, they are particularly likely to decline.

Young adults face an increasingly uncertain world. They are aware of what is going on in the world and many are wondering how they will be able to find a rewarding job and a pleasant life when so much chaos surrounds them.

Parents have all the usual worries of the world along with trying to ensure their children are safe and happy. Sometimes their children are bullied. This can be a very worrying time for child and parent alike and a troubling experience for all.

Many parents still worry about their grown-up children even after they have left home. They can also stress about any grandchildren that they might have. At the same time as this, they are facing their own aging process. This may affect their mobility and wellbeing.

Some people live alone and do not have children. Other people bring up children by themselves.

Some people feel shunned by society in some way, because they dare to be different.

We are all unique with our own life stories. There are times in life when we feel energised and content, and there are other times when we feel drained and down.

In the world of work, there are many times when people can feel as if they are fading. They can struggle to find work in the first place. All the rejection emails can be demoralising when applying for a job.

Once they get a job, they enter the world of work. They are introduced to office politics and sometimes even workplace bullying.

Many people work hard, but do not receive enough pay. This can lead to them feeling undervalued and they risk getting into debt.

There are opportunities to be promoted for some people. They may feel excited when they receive the promotion, only to find the job is more stressful than they anticipated.

People face financial pressures and health challenges. These experiences can be draining too.

Receiving appropriate help and support for these difficulties isn't always easy.

Some people experiment with drugs and alcohol. They may do this recreationally, or in an attempt to feel better. Drug taking can get out of control and further add to the difficulties of life.

Feeling stressed for a long period can lead to feeling washed out and exhausted. Many people are dragging themselves through life carrying all their worries on their shoulders and struggling to find a solution to their problems.

All this stress has a detrimental impact on mental health and can increase the likelihood of people becoming anxious and depressed. In turn, physical health can also become affected.

So many of us are feeling that we are fading away and struggle to know who to turn to for help.

What I have discovered is that the first thing we need to do is focus on ourselves.

What do I mean by this?

Well, we have been taught to focus our energies and efforts upon others and the external world, what we see going on around us. These are important areas, but we often forget to pay attention to ourselves and our needs.

I am not talking about being selfish and ignoring the needs of others, but I am suggesting that for us all to thrive on this planet we need to start showing ourselves some more love and care.

If we can learn how to love and care for ourselves, we will be in a better position to help and support others. That way, we can all stop fading and start living with happiness and purpose.

Read on to the next chapter where I introduce myself to you and explain how I figured out how to fix this fading process... (Spoiler Alert: I learnt the hard way!)

Chapter 2: Start With You.

I could have done with reading a book like this years ago. They say that you teach what you most need to learn, and I think this may well be true for me.

I am not a guru, I am no expert in this, but I have learnt from my own experiences.

I have looked into what I can do to improve things and as I try it all out, learning as I go, my intention has been to pass on the things that I have found useful in the hope that they can help you too.

This book explores the steps I have taken, am still taking, in my quest to stay vibrant and in full focus rather than fading away into the background.

I have decided to keep in all the failures and pitfalls that I have encountered, so that maybe you can avoid some of them yourself.

We want to live happy, healthy vibrant lives. It isn't always easy to live this way.

I truly believe this goal is attainable and there are specific actions that we can take to help bring about this positive change.

Let's return to the quiz for a moment:

Look back on the questions and how you scored in each area. This will provide you with clues about the areas of your life that you might wish to focus on now.

(By the way, I scored 7/7 when I first asked myself these questions. I think that my score shows how much I needed to find a way to stop fading and start shining.)

Let me tell you a bit more about me and how I came to notice all this fading stuff.

I have grown up kids, a caring job, I love to help people, and I enjoy giving. My life has been filled with exciting experiences and I am sure I have many more adventures to come.

Helping other people makes me feel good. If I am truly honest with myself, I often like to feel indispensable. I guess I am looking for evidence that I matter and that my being alive on this wonderful planet Earth has purpose.

It is great to feel needed, right?

Well, it is sometimes, a lot of the time even, but not always.

On my quest to help others, I often tell myself that it has to be me that makes the effort with people. Making sure I am checking in on others, is important to me. It helps me feel needed, that much is true, but at the same time I can sometimes resent it.

Can you relate to this?

When I was younger, I was much as I am now, but I think I was a bit more confident then. I enjoyed much of what I did including bringing up my kids, holding down challenging, rewarding jobs and spending time following my various hobbies and interests.

As I have got older, I have started to feel rather worn down, and sometimes it feels as if I am missing the boat. I have noticed that Society tends to favour the young. Older people have to work harder to receive positive attention.

At times I have felt side-lined and that my own needs were not being met.

I made up a rule that I had to be the one to stay in touch with people and if I didn't, I risked being forgotten. I didn't know why I thought like this. I didn't like feeling this way and so I started to wonder how I could turn this around.

Adverts on TV are filled with young, successful people and I couldn't help noticing older people are often used to advertise products such as wrinkle cream and denture glue.

Surely older people have more to offer than that?

I am not saying denture glue isn't useful. I am sure for many people, it is an essential purchase, but every person using denture glue has a rich life history and so there is so much more to them than the fact that they wear dentures.

Every person has lived their own unique life, so they have their individual story to tell if only people would listen to them.

Since I noticed myself starting to fade, I have been on something of a voyage of self-discovery. I have delved into self-help books and tried out exercises to help me feel better. In my quest I have tried out a lot of approaches and techniques. I have discovered what works for me and I have found out what doesn't really help me.

I have tried lotions, potions, exercise techniques, you name it. Some of them have been a lot more successful than others.

I would love it if you read this book, try out the suggestions that appeal to you and then email me with your opinions. I know we are all different and that what might work well for one person may not be as helpful for another. I can learn as much from your ideas and suggestions as you can learn from me.

Your feedback can be used to help me offer useful coaching books and sessions in future. Email me at: cathee@hotmail.co.uk Please make the title 'Stop Fading Away' so I can find your email in my inbox.

We can all learn from and inspire one another. I have learnt so much from other people. I admire celebrities on TV who use their fame to highlight important issues to help raise awareness.

In UK, at the age of 44, celebrity Davina McCall thought she was 'losing it' as she started to experience symptoms of the Menopause. After discovering many other women felt as she did, she decided to raise this issue by being involved in a Channel 4 programme 'Sex, Myths and The Menopause.' 2021

I think she did a wonderful thing in speaking out about her challenges, and there are many other brave, inspirational people, willing to share their own difficulties in the hope that this may help others.

In this book, my wish is to help you realise that there is nothing wrong with you. There are reasons why you feel worn down and exhausted and there are things that you can do to feel considerably better.

Who am I?

I'm Cathy. I am 54 years old.

As I said earlier, I wouldn't consider myself to be an expert or guru, but I think that's a good thing. It means that if I can do it, you can definitely do it. You don't have to be an expert on personal development to call a halt to the fading process and start turning up the colour and volume in your own life.

Let me tell you a little more about me.

I have been a project worker supporting adults with drug and alcohol problems, homelessness, and mental health challenges. I have also been a residential worker, a teaching assistant, a teacher, a Special Needs Coordinator and a Head Teacher.

I am now a wellbeing worker supporting children and young people who have communication and interaction difficulties. I have also trained as a life coach. I have written a number of personal development books which are available on Amazon.

That's a potted history of me.

I would love to hear more about you. You can email me or message me on my Facebook Coaching page:

https://www.facebook.com/profile.php?id=100048681623893

Over the years, I have met so many people who are both hardworking and caring. Like me, they have been feeling that they have little time for themselves.

Seeing so many people in a similar situation, I decided that something had to be done.

What could I do to help myself and help others?

I am finding the aging process has its challenges including a discovery that older women can feel rather invisible in Society. I am aware from talking to people of different ages and from different walks of life, that these feelings are not exclusive to women of my age.

Many people have been struggling with the way they are feeling and wishing that they could feel better.

I believe that there are no such thing as positive or negative emotions. We can have a belief that if we don't feel happy all the time that there is something wrong with us.

This belief can put a lot of pressure on us.

Feel your whole range of emotions. Try and recognise them and accept that they are there.

You are not bad or wrong for feeling angry, bored, or jealous.

You get to decide if you need to take any action in your life to help you feel less angry, bored or jealous.

Other people experience a full range of emotions too. They are responsible for their behaviour, and you are responsible for yours.

Worrying too much about what other people think of you isn't going to help you.

A lot of personal development focuses on how we feel about things. We think something and convince ourselves that what we feel is true.

If we feel a certain way, we tend to notice the emotion we are feeling reflected in what is happening around us. If we are feeling sad, we notice sad things happening. If we are feeling angry, we notice things that add to our anger. Other people seem to reflect back to us how we are already feeling. We do the same to them. If we feel happy, we smile, and this has a positive effect on people we pass, but when we are angry, we frown, and this can have a knock-on impact on the people we come across.

As I have illustrated earlier, getting older can increase self-doubt and reduce confidence in your own abilities. Trying to help others without leaving enough time for yourself can lead to you feeling worn out and out of balance. This means you have less energy to help others as well as yourself.

This book isn't only about getting older though. People of all ages can feel washed out by life.

I decided that there had to be a way to get more balance into my life and once I had figured that out, I could help others to achieve the same.

This book sets out what I have discovered.

It shows you what I now do to feel more balanced in my life.

Would you be willing to try a '30-Day Experiment?'

I almost forgot to tell you, as I write this book, I am carrying out a 30-day experiment myself. I will tell you more about that later.

I think that experiments are great.

You can try things out and see how they work for you.

As you read this, I challenge you to carry out a 30-day experiment too. I want this book to be practical, to help you to feel more balanced and content as soon as possible.

Let’s get started!

Find paper and a pen or type your answers. You will refer back to them later.

To begin with I would like you to decide how happy you are feeling right at this moment and give yourself a score out of 10. Write it down.

A 1 suggests that you are feeling very sad and a 10 indicates that you are extremely happy. You may feel something in between.

At the end of the experiment, in 30 days, you rate your happiness again and see if the score has improved.

At the start of my 30-day experiment, I rated my happiness at 7/10, that’s not too bad, right?

I think the excitement of actually deciding to write this book boosted my score to a 7, as lately I have been dragging along at around 5/10.

Trying things out and then evaluating how you feel, is a great way to start living a more vibrant, exciting life.

I find life is very much a series of experiments. We try something out and if we like it, we carry on doing it. If we try something and it doesn't work out, we can choose to try again or give up.

We learn so much from our life experiences.

You have completed the first step of the experiment. There is more to follow.

Now we are moving on to the importance of us asking for help when we need it:

I am thinking back on my life now. I would like to tell you about an experience I had around 30 years ago. It is an example of being stubborn and not being willing to ask for help.

When my children were little, I ran a playgroup. I loved taking them to the group to play with their friends. I raised money so we could go on outings and those trips were great fun. The trouble was, I found it extremely hard to ask for help. I would organise a barbeque on the hills by the sea. I would buy the food and haul it up the hill in an enormous rucksack not feeling able to ask anyone to help me carry the load. I would arrive at the venue, hot and bothered and try my best not to show how flustered I was feeling.

Looking back now, I am certain someone would have been more than willing to help me with the shopping and transportation of the food, all I had to do was ask. but I couldn't bring myself to.

Can you relate to this?

Neglecting your own needs has consequences, as I soon discovered.

One day, I was sitting in my flat watching TV when I started to feel very odd. I felt like my heartbeat was irregular and I had pins and needles moving around on my face. I was convinced that I was having a heart attack, so I went to the phone box and called 999. Few people had mobile phones in those days.

The ambulance arrived and took me to hospital. My heart was monitored, and I was told that I wasn't having a heart attack, but my blood pressure was on the low side, and they suggested that I made an appointment with my doctor as soon as possible.

I got a taxi home, hyperventilating all the while, and I became convinced that the hospital staff had missed something.

I managed to make a doctor's appointment and while seated in the waiting room, the horrible sensations came over me yet again.

I had visions of being sent back to hospital in another ambulance but when it came to my appointment, I was able to go into the waiting room and wait for the doctor. The doctor called me into her office and asked me what was wrong.

I described my symptoms, she looked at her notes and then she said a surprising thing to me:

‘I don’t think I know what is wrong, I know what is wrong as I suffer this too. You are having a panic attack.’

I was shocked at her words.

She went on to tell me that some people receive medication for the condition while others find alternative approaches including breathing into a paper bag when they are hyperventilating to help ease the situation.

I burst into tears. My doctor was so sympathetic and advised me to read around the issue and work out what strategies appealed to me.

I did just that.

I went to the shop, bought a book on panic attacks, and read the entire book in a few hours.

The book mentioned that up to 40% of people will have a panic attack at some point. I found this shocking as I didn’t know of anyone who had this condition.

My reading also suggested that some people who experience panic attacks do so because they have ignored or suppressed their emotions regularly. They didn't take enough time out to look after themselves.

The books suggested meditation and relaxation techniques as a remedy, and I decided to try this out. I listened to guided meditation, and it did help.

I did have a few more panic attacks but got better at recognising the early symptoms and was able to make sure I relaxed more.

I haven't had a panic attack for around 28 years. I have learnt how to recognise when I am feeling stressed, and I take action.

I started to talk to people about my experience and I was surprised to discover that quite a few people I know had them too but didn't usually like to talk about them.

There has long been a taboo around talking about mental health challenges, but I am glad to see that people are becoming more open these days.

Talking about your worries and challenges with the right people can really help.

It can be hard to admit that you need help and support.

Why is it so hard to ask for help?

We are going to look into this in more depth a little later.

Hopefully I have managed to establish that I definitely needed to work on asking others for help.

Is this something that you struggle with too?

In Chapter 3 we will have another look at those quiz questions and see what we can do to reduce our score, all in our quest to call a halt on the fading process.

Chapter 3: Answering The Quiz Questions.

Have a look at the answers you gave to the quiz.

Question 1.

Are you the kind of person who spends their time worrying about other people, hoping

they are O.K. and doing what you can to help them? Yes/No

Yes!

This shows that you are likely to be a kind and caring person. You want to help others when you can, and you are happy when things are going well for them.

Having empathy for others and a willingness to help them when needed, are good things.

It is like so many things in life, these qualities are good until they are taken to the extreme.

If you spend a lot of time worrying without taking any action to remedy the situation, you are likely exhaust yourself and all that worrying isn't going to help the other person.

If the person would like your help, you can help them to identify what challenges they face and they can start to explore possible solutions to these challenges.

The important thing is that they are the one who decides if they would like to change and that they would like your help.

They may be perfectly happy with things the way they are now. It may just be you that thinks that they have a problem.

The other thing is, that they may acknowledge that they do have a problem, but they would like to find a solution on their own and do not require your help.

It can be very hard to stand back and let people go their own way, but it is important to be clear on who would like your help.

You can make suggestions on possible actions that they can take to improve their situation, but ultimately it is them that gets to decide what actions they would like to take. You can offer to help, and they may accept your offer, but be careful not to take over and do things that you think might be in their best interests.

How do I know this?

I have discovered this through trial and error.

It can be tempting to make suggestions on what you think somebody else needs and then set about trying to 'fix' things the way you imagine they should be, but I have learnt that people need to decide for themselves what they need in their lives. It may be that they ask you for your opinion or ask you for help, but ultimately the way they choose to live their life is up to them.

2. Do you try and help friends and family whenever you can?

Yes!

I want my friends and family to be happy. You may well feel the same way about your friends and family. It is good to be willing to listen and to help when needed, but if you leap in and offer to help too often, they can become dependent on you and that isn't doing a lot for their independence.

Children learn so much from trial and error. It is tempting to do everything for them, but this stops them learning important life skills.

When my children were little, and I worked full time, I felt guilty and so I didn't ask them to tidy up after themselves or help me cook. I felt the need to wait on them. I realise now, that this didn't help them.

Luckily, they are both good at cooking and looking after their homes now but looking back, I could have let them do more around the house. It would have helped me, at the same time as teaching them important life skills.

3.Do you have a caring job? (Teacher, Nurse, Carer, Doctor etc.)

Yes!

If you have a caring job, you are likely to know a lot of people in a similar position to you. They may be trying their best to help and support the people that they work with. Again, there is nothing wrong with being helpful. The problem occurs if you try to step in and prop other people up without giving them the opportunity to resolve their own challenges if they can.

If every individual does their bit to help the team, things run smoothly. If you dash about trying to do everything yourself, you risk wearing yourself out.

4. Do you love helping others but end up leaving yourself with little time and energy to look

after yourself?

Yes!

The problem here is that we put all our efforts into helping other people and end up feeling drained. When we have our own challenges, we tend to ignore them and hope that they will go away while we focus our efforts on helping others. If we carry on like this, there is a danger that we will burn out.

5. Do you secretly wish that other people would notice how much you do, how busy you are

and offer to help you sometimes?

Yes!

The trouble with secretly wishing is that other people cannot read our minds. They don't know when we are struggling unless we let them know and we are willing to ask for help when we need it.

I know this can be very hard to do but it is really important. That help can come in the form of friends and family, or it may be that you realise that professional help is needed.

6. Do you feel worn out and even a bit resentful?

Yes!

When we get tired, it can be hard to keep the feelings of resentment at bay. We struggle on, doing what we can for others, but find that we are increasingly tired and stressed and that nobody else appears to have noticed that we are flagging.

We can secretly blame them for not noticing that we need help, but I have realised that communicating our needs to others is vital.

7. Do you feel guilty when you put yourself first?

Yes!

On the rare occasions when we do say ‘No’ and we put ourselves first, we can feel guilty and wish that we had agreed to help after all. Saying ‘Yes’ when you mean ‘No’ can become a habit. You end up agreeing to do things you don’t want to do but you feel resentful that yet again there you are rushing about after other people. No-one seems to have noticed that you have needs too.

If you look back at your answers to these questions just as I am doing, you will begin to see that there are some areas where you can begin to change your approach in order to achieve a more favourable outcome for everyone.

As you can see, if you scored highly in the quiz, you are likely to be spending your time doing all you can to help others. You are likely to be leaving so little time for yourself that you feel as if you are fading fast.

You may secretly resent people for not noticing that you need help, but I am here to tell you this has little to do with them, it's mostly about you.

You have the power to fix this.

You can learn how to say 'No' when you don't want to do something instead of reluctantly saying 'Yes.'

It is important that we consider The External World.

Recent events have certainly added to our stress!

Before we look into ways to stop fading, it is important to take some time to acknowledge what we have gone through recently. In fact, we are still going through it.

As well as running about after other people as we always have done, we have been trying to stay calm and helpful during a Global Pandemic.

As I write this, we are entering a hot summer in UK. Temperatures reached 40 degrees Celsius last week which is extremely hot for UK, and the News is reporting on wildfires raging in other parts of the world brought on by extreme heat. Many people are starting to worry if this is a sign of rapid climate change and are concerned about future generations.

We are making plans for holidays and are hoping that the holidays will be able to go ahead this year.

The last two summers have seen us planning to go on holiday and then having to cancel or postpone our plans. Weddings have been postponed and summer festivals cancelled.

The Covid Pandemic triggered Lockdowns throughout the world, and limited our ability to travel abroad.

Most of us have spent long periods of time at home, perhaps alone, wondering what the future would hold for us all.

With time on our hands, we can worry about the things that have gone wrong in the past and the things that might go wrong in the future. Worrying for long periods is exhausting. It is not surprising that many of us feel worn out.

There is talk of the Covid Pandemic worsening again and there are other viruses that we are told may also be a threat.

All kinds of negative scenarios can play out in our heads, and we can tend to blame ourselves for things that have gone or may go wrong.

The News keeps flashing up alarming headlines about war, illness, a cost-of-living crisis, and political scandals. All this chaos, added to the afore mentioned Climate Crisis is giving people sleepless nights.

You name it, we hear about it, and we worry about it.

Not only are we concerned about ourselves, we worry about our loved ones.

Whatever we do, whatever actions we take, we try our best to do things that makes the situation better, not worse. All too often, we fear that things are getting worse.

It is hard to stop worrying but there are some very helpful techniques that I have started to use that have been greatly helpful to me so I will share them with you.

Chapter 4: The Inner Critic.

In this chapter we discover our 'Inner Critic.' It is that voice in our head that points out our failures. It chatters away in the background offering us a running commentary of our failings. We can be strongly influenced by our inner critic. Here we begin to look at how destructive this can be.

If you add the impact of the inner critic to all the afore mentioned worrying, it is not surprising that we feel exhausted!

For some people, the voice of the inner critic can remind us of a disapproving teacher or family member who was critical of us when we were young.

Basically, this critic finds fault in more or less everything we say and do, and this can cause us to stop trying things rather than risk failure.

When we spend too much time listening to our inner critic, we treat ourselves more harshly than we treat others.

The inner critic pretends to be reality and sabotages us. What I mean by this is we believe that what the inner critic is saying must be true. This can make us feel like complete failures because we can't see that this critic isn't helpful or accurate.

It points out what it thinks we are doing wrong, and it tells us what we should be doing.

I have become wary of the word 'should.'

It can make us feel inadequate if we don't do something, but in reality, we don't have to do anything unless we wish to.

The word 'should' can be motivating at first, but soon becomes exhausting.

Later in this book, we will be exploring techniques to help us to quieten down the inner critic.

We have a tendency to take any old thought that pops into our head rather seriously. We think about something, and we start to focus our attention on that thought.

An example might be, 'The shops might run out of food supplies.'

This thought may well have been triggered by something you had been listening to such as a news report. Once that thought enters your head, you will probably start to worry. You can start to imagine all sorts of frightening scenarios where you arrive at the shop only to find empty shelves. You worry that you may run out of food and so you drive to the shop and start buying up everything in sight. Your thought triggered anxiety prompting you to go to the shop to ensure you have enough supplies. Your thought triggered a feeling which prompted this behaviour. You have acted upon this thought, without considering if the thought is true or false.

Once you go to the shop and find there are plenty of supplies, you start to feel better until the next thought enters your head.

Believing and acting upon every thought that enters your head can become exhausting.

Feelings are very useful, even the ones we regard as 'negative' such as sadness and anger.

There is also no such thing as positive or negative emotions. We can believe that if we don't feel happy all the time that there is something wrong with us. Experiencing the full range of emotions including sadness, happiness and joy is part of life.

I have had a tendency to suppress 'negative' emotions such as anger and sadness but now realise this doesn't help. Denying that you feel a certain way doesn't stop that feeling. It is likely to resurface despite your attempts to deny that it is there.

There is nothing wrong with any of us. When we get stressed, we can start to imagine all sorts of things about other people. We can think they don't like us or that they are angry with us, for example.

Other people are simply doing what we are doing, they are trying to get by. If they don't call you when you were expecting them to, it is unlikely to be because they don't like you. It is more likely to be that they were distracted by something else happening in their life.

American writer Mark Twain said, 'What other people think of me is none of my business.'

What did he mean by this?

I take his words to mean that it is best to be who you truly are without worrying about the opinions of others.

A lot of personal development focuses on how we feel about things. We think something and convince ourselves that what we feel is true. Two years ago, Hale Dwoskin's 'Letting Go- The Sedona Method Movie' came out. It is still available on YouTube.

I remember enjoying it and the main lesson I took away with me was something called the Triple Welcoming. The movie can explain this a lot better than I can, but essentially it reminds us to welcome how we feel instead of trying to suppress it. Welcome all the thoughts and feelings that you have about wanting to fix those feelings or push them away. You also welcome any sense that you have that it is personal. We can take things personally that really aren't personal to us.

Basically, this reminds me that if we can accept our feelings without trying to get rid of them, they have less of a stressful impact on us. It is also worth remembering that tough things happen to all of us at some point and if we can accept this too, we don't feel as if the universe is conspiring to ruin our lives.

If we feel a certain way, we tend to notice the emotion we are feeling reflected in what is happening around us. If we are feeling sad, we notice sad things happening around us. If we are feeling angry, we notice things that add to our anger. Other people seem to reflect back to us how we are already feeling. We do the same to them. If we feel happy, we smile, and this has a positive effect on people we pass but when we are angry, we frown and this can have a knock on impact on the people we come across.

Many of us feel uncomfortable when we experience some feelings. They tend to be the feelings that some people label as negative. These include feelings of sadness and anger. Feelings aren't really positive or negative. They are just feelings. They come and go.

We tend to underestimate the importance of breathing fully and deeply. When we feel something, and it makes us uncomfortable, instead of pushing the feeling away simply allow the feeling to be there and focus on your breath. Make sure you are breathing deeply. You don't need to fix anything, simply allow yourself to feel however you feel and keep focusing on your breath. The feeling will probably intensify. Keep breathing and wait until the feeling subsides by itself. When people do this, they may start yawning or feel tearful. This is fine. You are simply acknowledging your feelings and allowing them to be exactly as they are. Eventually they will go just as the clouds in the sky don't stick around forever.

Try this next time you experience a strong emotion and see how it works for you.

We have started to consider the power of thoughts and feelings.

How do we cope with those thoughts that keep on returning?

There is a solution that I have started using. It is working for me, so I am going to share it with you now.

Next time a thought enters your head and you become aware that you are having a thought, try acknowledging that it is just a thought and that thoughts come and go. Maybe the thought is true but maybe it isn't. Acknowledge the thought, accept that it is just a thought and then focus on your breath for a few minutes or take in the environment by using your senses. What can you see? What can you hear? What can you touch, taste or smell?

By doing this you have detached yourself from your thought and you can now analyse it in a calmer way.

What evidence do you have that the thought is true? You can spend time thinking of any evidence that you have that the thought could be true. After that, you can ask yourself what evidence you have that the thought might be false. Spend time thinking of any evidence that you have that the thought is false.

Noticing our thoughts is an important first step. Realising that not all the thoughts we have are true is a crucial next step.

Chapter 5: Problem Solving.

What can we do after we notice these thoughts?

Now you have the thought in a better perspective, you can begin to problem-solve. What actions can you take to improve the situation? There could be a number of actions that you can take. In the example above, you could have asked a friend if they had any evidence that stocks were getting low in shops before dashing to the shop to panic-buy. This might have reassured you that you didn't need to go shopping as the stocks were fine.

In some situations, there aren't really many actions that you can take to improve the situation but now you are feeling calmer and less triggered by your thought. That means that you can choose to do things you find relaxing or distracting to take your mind off things that you can't change.

Relaxation is such an important skill. I have neglected it at times in my life. I used to do yoga and meditation when my children were young, and I found the process relaxing. I then told myself I didn't have time for it as I was too busy doing other things. I realise now that this was a mistake.

'You should sit in meditation for 20 minutes each day unless you are too busy, then you should sit for an hour.' Zen Proverb.

Try and make time each day for relaxation and this is likely to have a positive impact on your wellbeing.

Have you heard about Mindfulness?

According to the Oxford Dictionary: Mindfulness is 'a mental state achieved by focusing one's awareness on the present moment, while calmly acknowledging and accepting one's feelings, thoughts, and bodily sensations, used as a therapeutic technique.'

Mindfulness is something that helps me to calm the inner critic and it helps me to be less reactive to some of the thoughts that enter my head.

A helpful mindfulness quote is from Sharon Saltzberg: 'Mindfulness isn't difficult, we just need to remember to do it. '

This is so very true. I am currently challenging myself to 30-days of mindfulness as I write this book. It is incredible how easy it is to forget that I am doing this, and I make up all sorts of excuses about why I haven't got time to do it.

Each time an excuse pops up, I gently but firmly dismiss it and make an effort to complete my 10 minutes of mindfulness.

I believe that the 10 minutes of invested time is well worth it. I am finding it easier to concentrate and I can write for longer bursts of time. As I write the first draft of this chapter, I am only 8 days into my experiment, and I am noticing benefits. I am writing a short blog on my Substack page, and this is helping me to chart my progress as I notice it.

The calmer I feel, the less seriously I take my inner critic and the easier it is to release some unhelpful thoughts. Try it for yourself and see how it works for you.

This is the next element to the 30-day challenge I have suggested to you.

The Mindfulness Challenge:

Set aside 10 minutes each day for the next 30 days. Sit somewhere comfortable and quiet. Close your eyes and focus on your breath. Make sure that you are breathing fully and deeply. Your thoughts and feelings will come and go as you do this. When you become aware of them, don't focus on them, simply let them be there and refocus on your breath.

Each minute seems to last for ages when you first start doing this. You can think the 10 minutes is almost up only to find you have only been focusing on your breath for just 3 minutes.

Don't worry, you will get better at it. Stick with it for 10 minutes for 30 days and see how this works for you. It is helpful to make a few notes of any key findings. You could set a timer to help you work out when the 10 minutes is up.

So now you have another element of the 30-day challenge to work on.

Now, think back to the happiness rating you gave earlier in the book.

Do you remember when I rated my happiness out of 10? I last did this a week ago and I was at 7/10.

Today I am at 8/10 partly because I am able to capture a lot of the ideas that I wanted to capture in this chapter and partly because schools break up in 2 days' time, so I am about to start my lovely long summer holiday.

How are you feeling at the moment? Rate how you feel out of 10 and see if the rating differs from your original rating.

The way you feel can be influenced by a number of key areas in your life. We will be looking at this further in the next chapter.

Chapter 6: Areas of life.

There are key areas of stress in our lives. We can worry about friends and family, our finances, our careers, our mental and physical health, our environment, our hobbies, our spirituality or religion. Some areas of our lives may be going well, while others may be contributing to our feelings of stress.

While we are in the habit of rating things, it can be useful to be aware of how we feel about each area of our life. We can rate each area out of 10. It might be that work is causing someone the most stress, so they award that area 3/10 while they love their home environment and rate it 8/10.

Rating each area can help us to identify how we are feeling overall, and which areas of life are giving us the most cause for concern. This can help us to begin to identify ways to improve the situation even a little bit.

I discovered this approach when I trained as a life coach around 7 years ago. It was one of the techniques I was encouraged to use with clients. I tried it out on myself, and it really helped me to see how each area of my life affects other aspects. If my finances are a source of stress, I may not be able to afford to go camping which is one of my favourite hobbies, for example.

If my home environment is a mess, then I don't find it easy to write. I look around thinking 'what a mess, I really should do something about this....'

I have found that looking at my life in this way can help me identify improvements I wish to make and that a little progress in one area can have positive knock-on effects on other areas.

It can help me realise that there is much that I can do to feel happier and less worn out. I realise that if I decide to spend an hour tidying up, my environment looks so much better and this helps me to settle down and focus on my writing, for example.

> I rate each area of my life out of 10 and then figure out what small actions I can take that would move my score in each area up by one point. It doesn't really matter which area I choose, taking action in this way can help me to see fairly rapid improvements.

Try this for yourself. It is a simple technique, but it is very effective, and it helps you realise that you have more control over your life than you may think you do.

Spend some time now rating the key areas of your life. This is the next part of your 30-day challenge.

I have recently rated my own life. This was at the end of a long term working in school, so I was feeling particularly tired.

These were my scores:

It is important to be honest with yourself and rate each area in a way that reflects the way you feel at the moment.

Friends and Family: 8/10 as things are going well for most of them and I hope to see most of them soon.

Finance: 6/10 The cost-of-living crisis is getting a lot of airtime on The News and this has triggered some anxiety.

Career: 8/10 I love my job.

Mental and Physical Health: 6/10 I need to strengthen my knee joint that has been affecting my mobility lately.

Environment: 5/10 My place needs a good tidy as I have been doing the minimum amount of housework possible as I have been so busy.

Hobbies: 6/10 My writing is going well but I would like to find time for Art.

Spirituality/Religion: 7/10 My Mindfulness Challenge is helping me to feel uplifted in this area.

These scores are interesting. They help me to take a snapshot in time. I can assess how I am feeling now and decide what actions I might like to take in each area.

I ask myself: 'What do I do to move the scores up by one point each?'

Friends and Family: To move from an 8 to a 9 I have arranged times to meet up with friends and family over the next month.

Finance: To move from a 6 to a 7 I am cutting back on fuel costs this week as I am spending a week at home tidying, writing and creating art.

Career: To move from 8 to 9 I have some training to participate in in September which is

likely to be useful.

Mental and Physical Health: To move from a 6 to a 7, I am carrying out daily knee strengthening exercises.

Environment: To move from a 5 to a 6 I am devoting the next couple of days to clearing up.

Hobbies: To move from 6 to a 7 I will do some Art after I have finished tidying up.

Spirituality/Religion: To move from a 7 to an 8 I will continue with my Mindfulness exercises and focus on deep breathing.

This exercise only takes a few minutes. Recording my intention in my diary helps remind me what I aim to do over the next few weeks.

Try this methoc for yourself. I find that making progress in one area can help me to feel motivated to make improvements in other areas too.

One area that affects our wellbeing is our relationship with others. This is greatly affected by the way we communicate. We will be looking at this in the next chapter.

Chapter 7: Communication

So far, we have looked at the inner critic and the way thoughts pop into our heads and can get taken far too seriously. We have examined ways to act on problems as well as release the things that we can't control.

Now we are going to look at the important area of communication. Communication is vital if we are to let others know how we are feeling.

Communication is an important skill, and if we are unable to clearly communicate other people struggle to understand our needs.

Lack of effective communication can add to our stress and feelings of exhaustion.

In fact, the way we communicate with others can contribute to or reduce our stress.

Communicating With Children:

Young children are learning to speak and listen. They can become easily frustrated and need adults to communicate with them using simple language. It can be exhausting trying to explain things to a toddler having a tantrum.

Older children can become more argumentative, and they can challenge your ideas, views and opinions. This can be hard to deal with.

Teens start to value the opinions of friends and people living outside of their home. This can lead to arguments and stress.

Grown up kids learn how to find their own way in life. Some may still live at home, while others move away. They may adopt a different lifestyle and hold different views to you. This can be challenging for many.

Colleagues And Clients:

Colleagues at work can he hard to communicate with. They may be in a position of authority over you, or you may be in a position of authority over them. This can lead to a conflict of interests. Each work environment has its own culture. Some people fit in better than others. Feeling left out at work can be very stressful.

Clients can also be challenging to communicate with. They may want you to respond to them whenever they feel they need you while you try to maintain some boundaries and are reluctant to be contacted at weekends, for example.

Communication Tips:

Active listening can help with communication. If you fully listen to someone instead of mentally preparing a response while they are talking, they are likely to feel heard and more willing to listen to what you have to say. I tried this out and found the improvement remarkable. How on earth do people know we are fully listening rather than mentally rehearsing a response or waiting for a gap in conversation so we can share our own ideas and suggestions?

Another thing I have figured out the hard way is the need to choose the right time to let someone know how we are feeling. You might be in the mood to talk but they may be distracted. This is unlikely to work out well. If you explain that you would like to talk with them and ask when a good time for them is, they are more likely to communicate more effectively with you.

Another reason we struggle to get our needs met and our voices heard is we have spent a long time listening to other people's needs and doing what we can to help them. We might offer good advice and suggestions but rarely ask for help and support from others. People can get used to this and may not realise that you need help unless you are able to communicate this to them.

It can be hard to accept help if you consider yourself to be an independent person, but we all need help sometimes. In the next chapter we will be thinking more about this area.

Chapter 8 Independence:

If you are the kind of person who tries to help others, it can be tempting to do everything for them and not give them the opportunity to try things for themselves. It is good to be supportive, but if you never let someone try something for themselves, they will never become independent.

We all learn a lot from trying and failing. While failing can hurt, it is an essential part of learning.

The other problem we have is we can feel a lot more comfortable being the helper rather than being willing to ask for help.

It can be hard to ask for help when you need it. You may prefer to be in the driving seat and be the one who fixes things, but we all need help sometimes. Never being willing to let others help you can rob them of the pleasure of being the kind and helpful one.

Another thing givers struggle with is letting others know how we really feel. We get asked if we want to do something and end up saying ‘Yes’ when we really want to say ‘No.’

It can also be hard to say ‘No’ when people ask you for something, but sometimes saying ‘No’ is the right thing to do.

Assertiveness is a useful skill to have here. Considering what people say and then giving them a clear, honest response can be valuable. If you feel someone is being unfair to you, finding a way to calmly and clearly communicate this to them can be very helpful.

I have found it hard to say ‘No’ to people in the past.

I didn’t think I could do this, but I tried it and it worked.

I have a family, I love them and try my best to be there for them.

I have kids who have grown up.

I take a real interest in what is going on in their lives and always hope they are enjoying themselves.

I find it much easier to be the listener and the helper. I struggle with asking them to listen to me or help me. I am getting better at this though. I have gradually felt more willing to be honest with them about how things are going in my life and realise that they are perfectly capable of giving me useful advice and support if I need it.

I have had a number of caring jobs where I have met many caring people. Listening to them has helped me to realise I am not alone, there are many people like me who care for others but struggle with allowing others to care for them.

I like to help people and enjoy giving. I imagine you do too. There is nothing wrong with that. Being caring and giving is a good thing but we must be willing to let other people give to us and help us when needed.

We have spent some time considering the importance of communicating our needs to others. Now we will look at other ways to make sure our needs are met.

Chapter 9: Why Do We Feel Like We Are Fading Away?

It can feel like we are fading away when our needs are not being met.

Older women in modern times can often feel that way. Our society places a lot of importance on people being young, fit, and attractive. This doesn't just apply to older women; it is something that many people feel.

If you are starting to feel old, unfit, and less attractive you can start to feel side-lined and ignored.

If you are a busy parent or carer with no time left for yourself, what can you do?

If work is draining you, or the struggle to make ends meet is causing you stress, how can you resolve this?

People from all walks of life can feel like they are fading.

How can we turn this around?

How can we feel like we are 'firing on all cylinders' once again?

Mindfulness can offer us all a solution.

We have started to look at Mindfulness as part of our 30-day challenge.

Let's explore it a little further now.

One of my favourite Mindfulness quotes has to be: 'Almost everything will work again if you unplug it for a few moments. Including you. '

This is taken from Lindsey O'Connor's 'Digital Nomad' podcasts.

If you think about it, they are right about electronic gadgets. If in doubt, turn the gadget off and then on again and that usually sorts out most problems. I love the idea of this applying to us. If you spend a few minutes each day unplugging yourself from your thoughts, you will feel much more light-hearted.

We can start by learning to put ourselves first. I know this sounds strange but once we start putting ourselves first, other people start to treat us differently.

Taking time out for Mindfulness is an example of putting yourself first.

Making improvements starts with you. You can start by being willing to examine the inner critic that we looked at earlier.

What are they saying?

Challenge the thoughts and work out how true they are. What evidence do you have that they are accurate? What evidence do they have that they might not be true?

Once we stop getting too sucked in by what the inner critic is saying we can start to feel better about ourselves. We can start to tune in to what we need.

Ask yourself, what do I need?

It can be hard to do this when we have been trained by society to think about what other people need, what they need from us.

Spend some time now really thinking about what you need.

Examine the areas of life. In what areas are things going well? In what areas are things rather stressful and in need of improvement?

Spend time asking yourself, what steps can you take to make some improvements?

Learning how to put yourself first isn't easy but you can learn to do it!

When you struggle and feel alone, think 'what advice would I give a good friend?'

Take that advice.

You can also imagine what would a good friend suggest that you do?

The responses you come up with might turn out to be helpful actions that you can take.

Listen to others and they will start to listen more fully to you. I have tested this out and it works.

How do you feel when people don't listen to you?

If you are anything like me you feel hurt, pushed out or side-lined but you are unlikely to let them know that this is the way you are feeling.

Why don't we let people know when we are feeling annoyed?

I suspect it is fear of rejection. If we tell someone we are not happy with something that they have said or done, we run the risk of them turning on us or walking away.

Next time someone ignores you, would you be willing to try something different? Would you be willing to let them know how you feel when they ignore you?

You could start by saying, 'When you don't listen, I feel...'

You then explain how you felt when they didn't listen to you.

It is scary starting to communicate your needs when you are not used to it, but the experience can be a lot more rewarding than you may think.

When someone disagrees with you, but they have been willing to listen to your point of view, they show that they are able to shift their perspective. This leads to greater understanding. This leaves the way open for the pair of you to compromise. You can say what you want, they can say what they want, and you can negotiate an agreement that both of you feel happy with.

There are a lot of actions we can take to improve many aspects of our lives and the way we communicate with others.

There are some things that we have little or no control over and these things can be the most stressful of all.

In the next chapter we will look at ways of coping with the things that we can't control.

Chapter 10 Acceptance:

Accepting things as they are can lead to us feeling a lot calmer and happier. We can spend so much time worrying about things that we can't control. Once we realise that the things that we are worrying about aren't things we can change, it is worth accepting this and finding a way to let go of all the concerns that we are holding onto.

Relaxation and distraction are both good ways to do this.

I think this quote is well worth considering: 'If it's out of your hands it deserves freedom from your mind too.' Ivan Nuru, Declutter Your Mind.

We have looked at some ways we can declutter our minds. We have briefly touched upon Mindfulness.

'Mindfulness gives you time. Time gives you choices. Choices skillfully made, lead to freedom.'

This wonderful quote is by Bhante Henepola Gunaratana. Their books are written clearly and plainly so they are easy to understand.

If you think about what is being said here, we have a good reason why mindfulness is worth your time. You put a few minutes a day into being mindful and this helps you to focus more on the present. This allows you to get things done. You think more clearly and are more decisive. This means you tend to make good choices. When it says your choices lead to freedom, I think that means freedom from feeling trapped. You feel less bogged down by things that you feel have gone wrong and you are not as preoccupied by things that could go wrong in the future.

When you are truly living in the moment you are free from all of that. You experience a sense of lightness and freedom.

I think Mindfulness encourages Acceptance.

'Mindfulness is awareness without criticism or judgement.'

This is a great quote by Jan Chozen Bays who writes about the benefits of mindful eating.

Mindful eating involves fully focusing on what you are eating without being distracted by other things.

It can be hard to be aware without criticising what you are thinking about but every time you notice yourself being critical you can gently let those thoughts go. We live in a rather judgemental society. When someone does something, critics are usually waiting in the wings to say that they did it wrong.

We judge ourselves and we judge others. When we notice ourselves doing this, we can let go of the judgements without being critical of ourselves for judging!

I can't resist another Mindfulness quote at this point:

'Mindfulness is simply being aware of what is happening right now without wishing it were different. Enjoying the pleasant without holding on when it changes. (Which it will.) Being with the unpleasant without fearing it will always be this way. (Which it won't.)'

James Baraz co-author of 'Awakening Joy.'

Accepting that happy moments pass is something I struggle with. Sometimes I have a lovely time cuddling my cat or dog and catch myself thinking, they won't be alive forever. I feel sad when I think of this and realise that focusing on that unknown time in the future when my lovely animals will die is spoiling the time that I have with them right now.

On the other hand, when something challenging or upsetting is happening it can be comforting to remember that this unpleasantness won't last forever.

Everything changes, nothing stands still.

Next, we will look at ways to cope with life's changes. We will find ways to feel more balanced.

Chapter 11: Balance.

In the quest for greater balance in my life I feel that I am making progress, but I am not perfect. I am quite a few steps closer to where I want to be, and my wish is that after you have read this book you will find yourself making progress too.

If you think about it, we are all in this together. We all have challenges and stresses. We are trying to do the best we can.

We go through life helping others and hoping to experience happiness ourselves.

Our lives can feel out of balance when we focus too much on one area and ignore other areas of our life.

If we are able to give some attention to those neglected aspects of our lives, we are better able to restore balance into our lives and we will begin to feel better.

I am thinking about life from the perspective of myself, an older woman living in UK. Older women can feel that society has started to pass them by.

The truth is there are many other groups and individuals who are struggling too.

Young people experience considerable peer pressure, workers have serious concerns about the current cost of living crisis – each group in society has their own worries. there's a lot to worry about.

Society has become increasingly divided. Some people are rich, and others are poor. It can be hard to find common ground and know what we can do together to create a better world.

We have all gone through a global pandemic which has impacted us all in different ways.

Children were asked to stay home from school so didn't meet their friends,

Some parents worked through the pandemic as 'essential workers' while others lost their jobs.

Some people are still working from home two years later. This has meant that we have all gone through a period of rapid adjustment and many of us have found the experience unsettling.

Opinion has been divided over global warming, the war in Ukraine, you name it.

There have been protests, government scandals and watching it all on The News can be draining.

We can feel overwhelmed when we try and take it all in.

It is helpful to be able to decide what are the things that we can do something about and what things that are out of our control?

One approach we can adopt in order to let go of overwhelm and regain balance is to begin to practice Mindfulness. I expect you knew I was going to say that didn't you?

Does Mindfulness even work?

This is a question that many researchers have been asking themselves.

I have read studies indicating how Mindfulness has helped many people, but I have heard of researchers suggesting that it doesn't always work.

This is the same with most methods and approaches. What works brilliantly for one person may work less well for others as we are unique.

In UK there was a recent study that suggested that giving teenagers Mindfulness lessons at school doesn't make much difference.

Apparently, pupils who took part in a trial said they weren't that interested and so few did the homework sessions they were asked to do.

Teachers and pupils in 85 schools took part in the study and the findings were published in Evidence Based Mental Health Journal. 2022

Researchers concluded that Mindfulness may help some pupils but offering it to all as lessons is unlikely to benefit everyone. Teachers apparently found the Mindfulness sessions more helpful.

I found out about this study while writing about Mindfulness in this book.

I found it a little disheartening, but then I considered that Mindfulness may not be something you can easily teach as standard lessons in school. It may lend itself better to parents and carers who find Mindfulness helpful introducing aspects of it to their children as part of their way of life.

It might be hard to convince a class of teenagers that Mindfulness is worthwhile as they may be influenced by their peers and the slow pace may not compete favourably with more active approaches such as PE.

We have established that Mindfulness may not appeal to everyone, but I would suggest that it definitely has its place in helping many of us to cope with the pressures of modern-day life.

Will Mindfulness help us cope with overwhelm?

We won't know unless we try.

Let's find out together.

If it doesn't work for you there are alternative approaches that you can try. We will touch on those later.

My research into the benefits of Mindfulness has served as a great reminder that there are many tools and techniques and that finding something that works for you is the most important thing.

As I mentioned earlier, I am carrying out the 30-day Mindfulness experiment as I write this book. I am fully committing to 10 minutes of Mindfulness each day and I am recording my findings in my Substack blog.

I would encourage you to try Mindfulness daily and record any findings.

Try Mindfulness, record your findings in a diary or journal and after the 30 days decide if it helps you or not. As I write this, I am 27 days into my experiment, and I am finding it to be an extremely positive experience.

I realise that I need to put the work in over a period of time to notice any difference.

It can be hard to commit to things as we all live such busy lives.

In order to give something a fair trial, it is important to try to stick with it.

If you think about it, some people find going to the gym to be motivating and helpful. They sign up and go every week. Other people sign up, try it a few times and then abandon it.

Why is this?

It may be that if they tried the gym regularly for a longer period of time, they would start to notice the benefits. Alternatively, it may be that going to the gym isn't appealing to them and they might prefer another activity such as swimming or dancing.

Our society likes things to be easy. If there was a pill that we could take that magically improved things, many of us would opt to take that pill regardless of cost or side effects.

I am not saying that pills don't have a place. Many people have conditions that are greatly helped by the right medication. What I am suggesting is that some alternative techniques take more time, effort and commitment and this can put people off.

I am thinking of the afore mentioned Mindfulness study. I am imagining a stressed teenager going to school, being put on a 10-week Mindfulness course and being asked to do some of the work at home. If they have never tried anything like this before they may find it strange or even boring. If their family are not committed to Mindfulness, they may not feel it necessary to encourage their teen to do their homework. If they did try the technique every day as they were encouraged to do, they may have found it to be more beneficial than they expected.

Mindfulness has been found to help some people cope with pain management.

Around 25% of the adult population live with chronic pain. This is pain that doesn't go away despite medication or treatment. Some people living with this have tried Mindfulness and found it to be a good distraction from their pain. This would be an incentive for them to keep up a Mindfulness practice. If they experience less pain while focusing on Mindfulness, then they are likely to continue.

If you keep an open mind and decide to try Mindfulness and it works for you then you have found a technique that costs nothing and you can use it at any time.

If it works for you then you might let others know about it in the hope that it may help them.

That is one of the main reasons for me writing this book.

We are all trying to find ways to cope with the pressures of life and if something works and is free to use then it is worth letting as many people know about it as possible.

If parents find Mindfulness helpful, they may try and find a way to encourage their children to try it.

Children may not be willing to sit for 10 minutes focusing on their breath, but they may be willing to play a game using their senses. Parents could ask their young children to sit for a minute and listen to all the sounds in their environment. After one minute their child can let them know what they have heard. The parent could play 'I spy' with their child.

They might say, ‘I spy with my little eye something beginning with C.’

The child looks around them naming things that they can see that begin with the letter C until they guess the correct item. Younger children may prefer to adapt this to ‘I spy with my little eye, something the colour red.’ They look around for red items and try and identify the object their parent has been describing.

These activities are mindful as the child is focusing on what is going on around them rather than worrying about things.

Children can be encouraged to use their other senses too in a similar way. They could be asked to taste two different flavour crisps and indicate which they prefer. This is using their sense of taste. There are similar activities that can be adapted to make use of the sense of smell and touch.

A young child can be asked to pick up a pinecone and describe how it feels or they can indicate which plant in the garden smells nicest. These activities invite children to use their senses and can be the foundation for teaching Mindfulness to them.

Older children can be distracted from their thoughts by being asked to listen to music, for example.

If parents and carers benefit from Mindfulness, they can be open with their children about this and their children are likely to be more willing to trying it for themselves if they know that it helps their loved ones.

Once you have come to the end of the 30-day Mindfulness experiment, you can decide if it is something that you may wish to continue.

If Mindfulness doesn't work for you, then maybe running or walking in the country may work better. Being outdoors, going out into Nature has many benefits.

There is a Japanese practice called Shinrin Yoku, or forest bathing. This basically involves going into woodland and being guided by someone trained in the method. This approach started in Japan in 1980's and research has indicated that it is good for physical and mental wellbeing. It helps people feel happier and more creative. It can lower heart rate, boost the immune system and speed recovery from illness.

This is an approach that I would like to try as I always feel calmer and more relaxed when I am in a forest.

Some people find cold water swimming, dance, yoga or running to be enormously helpful.

Exercise and being outside is not for everyone.

Other people find making music or art can free their mind while others find an invigorating shower or relaxing in a bubble bath really helps.

Anything that helps you to feel calmer and more balanced is worth trying.

Once you have found a way to clear your mind of all the worry circulating around in your head you are in a better position to identify the actions you can take to make some improvements in your life.

Finding balance in our busy lives is so important. When our mind is clear we make better decisions.

As part of the 30-Day Challenge, I would like you to do something for yourself each day. Take a few minutes to do something you really enjoy. At the end of this book is a list of possible suggestions. Some of these ideas may appeal to you while some may not. You decide what to do but the important thing is to commit to doing something nice for yourself every day.

Make a note of any thoughts and feelings that you have after doing these activities.

When our own needs are met, we are likely to feel balanced. This helps us to be clear on what actions we can take to bring about further positive change.

In the next chapter we will touch upon the benefits of clarity.

Chapter 12 Clarity:

Having a clear mind can help you to make wise decisions about when you can help others and when you might need to ask for help yourself.

Being clear on your own needs, knowing who and how to ask for help and being able to identify when you are able and willing to help others are important skills to have.

As we have considered, being able to communicate clearly and assertively is also important.

It is useful to have the ability to look at areas of your life and clearly assess what you are happy with and where you would like improvements to be made.

There is a lovely word, 'equanimity- it describes our ability to stay balanced regardless of the ups and downs of life.

If we can manage this, we allow ourselves to step off the roller-coaster of emotions that we usually experience.

It is inevitable that life is full of joys and sorrows. It can be tempting to live for the happy moments and shut out the sad ones but suppressing our emotions isn't good for us.

Being willing to accept things as they are can really help us develop a good sense of wellbeing.

Mindfulness assists us with this.

When you become aware that you are feeling low, a few minutes focusing on your breath or taking in your surroundings can help you to feel lighter, more carefree.

There are other steps that we can take to support our wellbeing.

These long-term strategies include making sure that you eat well, exercise and drink water.

It can be hard to make the effort to prioritise our wellbeing, but it is vital to long term mental and physical health that we are willing to treat ourselves well. If we keep neglecting ourselves because we are so focused on helping others, we will soon run out of energy and be unable to help anyone.

There are people that uplift us, and it is great to spend time with them.

When we are around some people, we feel restored and energised while other people can be mentally draining and demanding.

Spending time with people who are good for our wellbeing is time well spent.

Let us consider our health further. We will think about this in the next chapter.

Chapter 13: Good Health

What is Health?

We often focus on physical or mental illness when we think about our health.

Health is more than an absence of illness.

In 1947 the World Health Organisation (WHO) defined health as -'a state of physical, mental and social wellbeing.'

As we have considered, keeping ourselves physically well involves eating a good diet, drinking enough water, sleeping enough, and getting enough exercise.

How do we ensure a good state of mental wellbeing?

WHO defines this as 'a state of wellbeing in which every individual realises his or her own potential, can cope with the normal stresses of life, can work productively and fruitfully, and is able to make a contribution to her or his community.'

This is a wonderful definition and reminds us that mental wellbeing is more than a lack of mental illness.

How can someone realise their own potential?

In order to realise your potential, you need to have willpower and courage to work on goals that help you to achieve what you wish to achieve.

If you manage to complete this 30 -Day challenge, you will have demonstrated both willpower and courage.

What do you want from your life?

You can use your potential to work towards achieving that. You can identify steps you can take towards achieving your goals and reward yourself when you reach important milestones. You learn a lot from failure as well as success. The fear of failing can put a lot of people off trying, but if you are willing to keep trying, you have a much higher chance of success.

Coping with the 'normal' stresses of life is hard enough, but lately we have been coping with unprecedented situations. All our lives have been filled with uncertainty around the pandemic, the war in Ukraine and the cost-of-living crisis.

Adopting a solution-focused approach to life can help us cope with life's pressures.

We can be clear on what the challenges are, we can take time to consider possible solutions and then try one solution that we think might work. We can review any actions we take and consider if there is another action we can take if our first solution doesn't work as well as we had hoped.

The ability to work productively and fruitfully is another important element. In our society people tend to value well-paid jobs and some people who work voluntarily or for low wages can feel that they are not appreciated. This seems unfair to me as there are many unpaid and low paid roles that are crucial to the smooth running of society.

If you enjoy your work, you are likely to feel more fulfilled even if the pay is low. Knowing you make a difference to other people is rewarding to many people.

Making a contribution to our community is good for our wellbeing.

This contribution can take many forms including voluntary work.

What further steps can we take to support our wellbeing?

We will explore this in the next chapter.

Chapter 14: Wellbeing

We have talked quite a lot about the need to achieve balance in our lives. For a person to have good mental wellbeing they need to ensure their needs are met.

What further steps can we take to ensure this?

Now we will spend some time looking at our environment, occupation and any spiritual factors that impact on our lives. These areas contribute to our sense of wellbeing.

When our lives are balanced, we achieve a feeling of harmony.

What brings about harmony varies from person to person.

Some people find spending time online to be relaxing and enjoyable while other people find too much screen time adds to their lack of wellbeing.

As we have discovered, there are key areas in our lives that are most important to us and by doing what we can to ensure that our needs are met in these areas we can cope with the ups and downs of life.

We sometimes neglect key areas and if this happens, we can feel a sense of discord in our lives.

When we get out of balance in this way, we can look at the key areas of our lives and see what actions we can take to redress the things.

Focusing for a while on one area can benefit other areas. This means that we can choose to prioritise the areas that we relate to most. If our actions have a positive impact in that area, we are more likely to feel able to address other areas that need some attention.

What is social wellbeing?

Social wellbeing involves us having a sense of belonging and making a contribution to a community.

What is Community?

Community can be where you live, your family or friendship group. It can be a club you attend with people you relate well to.

If you are able to spend time with your community and work with them on commonly agreed goals, you are likely to experience a strong sense of social wellbeing.

Many people feel cut off from others and do not feel part of a community.

If this applies to you then there are steps that you can take to help you feel part of something.

It may be that you live on your own and can't get out of your home much. It might be that you live far away from the people you know and do not feel that you have much in common with the people around you.

If you can reach out and find people who are like-minded you are likely to feel less alone.

Think about the things that you enjoy doing and consider how you can connect with people who share your interests.

There may be a club you can join where people share similar hobbies to you. The club may be in your local area, or you may find an online community that you can become a part of.

It can be daunting taking those first steps to joining a new group or community but if you are brave and willing to try things you are likely to find some people that you can relate to.

Certain activities engage us, and we find them enjoying and fulfilling. Other activities are less enjoyable to us.

What energises and what depletes us?

This will vary from person to person. For some people going for a run will energise them while for another person, a chat with a friend can have a similar impact.

If we are willing to try new things, we might find an activity that greatly benefits our wellbeing.

As we are all unique the things that energise us are different. The things that deplete us also vary.

It can be helpful to spend a week noting down your existing activities and rating them according to the way they make you feel. This can help you work out if there are any changes you need to make to help your life feel more balanced.

I realised that one of the reasons I have been feeling worn out is that I have been neglecting my environment lately. I have been distracted by other things and the place started to look worn out and untidy.

When I decided to tidy up, I discovered that I had forgotten to water some plants and their leaves have dried out. They looked how I felt!

I can look at one of the neglected plants and regard it as a metaphor for the way I sometimes look after myself.

I am in a great position at the moment as I have had time to take care of my environment and myself. Tidying up and looking after the plants helps me to feel better, more energetic.

As soon as I tidy up and my plants look happier, I start to feel more creative. When my environment is neglected, I feel drained, it is as simple as that.

Balancing my time is key to living a fulfilled life.

The same will apply to you.

If you are feeling more tired than usual, you may find that one or more areas of your life are dragging you down.

If you spend time looking at each area of your life you may find that taking some action in those areas will lead to you feeling happier in general.

I don't know what stage you are at in your 30-Day challenge but if it is nearly complete, I imagine that there have been some days where it has been hard to stick to the Mindfulness session.

We can start out with good intentions and then we get distracted by life and we risk abandoning the activities that we intended to do. Things are often harder when we start off. Once things become a habit, they are easier to stick to. We are going to look at this further in the next chapter.

Chapter 15: Habits.

We develop habits over time. Some are regarded as good. They help us to stay healthy. An example of this could be the habit of regularly drinking water.

Other habits can be regarded as bad. One example might be drinking too much alcohol. While we know this is a bad habit, we can find it hard to stop drinking to excess. We feel bad for doing it and yet we find it hard to stop.

At this point it is helpful to remind yourself that habits form for a reason. If we are drinking too much on a regular basis, this habit will have been established as it serves us in some way.

When you find that you have adopted a bad habit, ask yourself what it is about this particular behaviour that serves you?

If you can work out how this habit serves you, then you can identify a healthier habit to replace the bad habit.

In the drinking alcohol example, you may realise that drinking helps you feel more relaxed and confident when mixing with people.

Once you realise this, you can identify other ways to feel relaxed.

Meditation and progressive muscle relaxation are techniques that can help with this.

Progressive muscle relaxation is when you sit in a relaxed position and then tense and relax one muscle at a time until you feel less tense.

Meditation takes many forms. Mindfulness meditation is the form mentioned in this book, but you might like to try other forms of meditation. Guided meditations are available on YouTube so you could choose one that appeals to you.

If you are able to find a good habit to replace a bad habit, you are likely to feel better over time.

It is a positive step to establish some good habits into your life.

Some activities appeal to you while others won't. See if you can identify some healthy activities that may uplift and energises you.

See if you can develop a good habit to replace a bad habit.

Some people find running does this, other people enjoy craft.

When I am feeling overwhelmed, I tell myself I don't have the time or energy to write or draw and paint. The truth is that if I devote even a few minutes to these pastimes I feel more energised and optimistic.

When we catch ourselves saying we haven't got time to do the things we enjoy, this is a sign that our life is sliding out of balance and that we need to take action to remedy this.

If we can find things to inspire us, we are more likely to stay on track.

In the next chapter we will be looking at some sources of inspiration.

Chapter 16: Inspiration.

We can learn a lot from Buddhism.

In Buddhism they mention the 'Four Immeasurables.'

Sujiva in 2007 described them as 'loving-kindness, compassion, appreciative joy and equanimity '

Our modern term for loving-kindness is friendliness.

Compassion is our willingness to end the suffering of others.

Appreciative joy is feeling happy for others and equanimity is experiencing feelings of calm based on the wisdom we have gained.

Sujiva is a Malaysian Buddhist monk. You don't have to be a Buddhist or a monk to gain from adopting elements of this approach.

Tonglen is a meditation practice that combines meditating on loving-kindness with meditating on compassion

It can be focused on yourself and on others. Breathing in and acknowledging your worries, pain or suffering and then exhaling your wish for compassion for yourself and others.

Wishing happiness and love for yourself and others can help you to feel lighter and more carefree.

This form of meditation isn't for everybody as some people can feel distressed at the thought of the pain and suffering of others.

Like with any practice, if something isn't helping you, stop doing it.

We are all so different so what can be uplifting for one person can be less effective for another.

The essence of Tonglen, is to be compassionate. You are encouraged to be compassionate towards yourself. This helps you to be happier and more resilient. This enables you to feel more awake and energised.

Buddhism offers us useful insight into suffering.

The Buddhist Four Noble Truths suggests that our suffering is self-imposed. We believe things should be different than they are. This can lead to challenge and pain which can add to suffering.

We are responsible for our own suffering, but we have the power to end it.

Buddhists suggest that we adopt 'The Middle Way.'

This approach consists of 8 steps that we can take. It is regarded as a slow, consistent way to improve our lives.

I am no expert in any of this, but I find it fascinating that there have been techniques and approaches that support wellbeing that were formulated many years ago.

Buddhists refer to:

Right view- which is our need to see where we are going.

Right Intention- once we know our path, we can decide to follow it.

Right speech- is where we ensure that what we say does not cause harm.

Right action- this is ensuring that what we do doesn't harm anyone or anything.

Right livelihood- is how we choose to live each day.

Right effort- is us fully focusing on what we are doing.

Right mindfulness- involves us considering the impact that we have on ourselves and others.

The eighth element is:

Right concentration- which ensures we are focused on what we are doing.

If we all lived by these principles, I have a feeling the world would be a better place.

Things can feel rather chaotic for us now, but things don't always have to stay like this.

Life is beautiful and rich, but everything eventually comes to an end or dies.

This can be hard for us to accept.

Why does life turn into death?

Everything is transient.

Life changes at every moment.

Bodies decline, relationships change. This is all part of the ebb and flow of life.

We find it hard to accept this.

Resisting doesn't help.

We may slow down as we age, but we also develop wisdom.

Wanting things that we cannot have can cause us distress.

Our desires can own us.

If we can understand and accept that all emotions are fleeting, life becomes easier.

Good experiences as well as bad stuff ends eventually.

We can learn how to make wise choices when it comes to expressing our feelings.

We can choose to pause first.

We can consider what we wish to say and when we are ready, we can say it.

Sometimes we take ourselves too seriously.

Buddhists believe that the self you know isn't real. We have roles.

We are in constant flux.

That makes sense to me. We behave one way around our friends, and we may behave differently around family or work colleagues.

Buddhists suggest that our current environment is a product of our previous thoughts and actions. What we think and do now can change our future.

This also adds up to me. In the example I gave earlier, I was feeling worn out and so I neglected my environment and some of my plants died.

When I realised that I was neglecting my environment, I chose to tidy it up and look after the surviving plants.

My environment is now more uplifting to me, and I feel that this is one of the factors that has supported my ability to get this book written.

Author Chris Niebauer, has written a number of books including one called 'No Self, No Problem.'

He suggests that neuropsychology is catching up to Buddhism and is willing to accept that our sense of self that is often referred to as the ego is an illusion conjured up by the left side of our brain. He speaks of the illusory self.

The left brain is said to be the logical part of the brain, so I imagine that creating the ego is its attempt to make sense of what is happening in the world.

I find this fascinating.

The reason I mention it here is to serve as a reminder not to take the ego too seriously!

I often consider:

Where do thoughts come from?

Where do they go?

We tell ourselves stories to explain what we think is happening in the world. These stories may not be factual, but they feel real to us.

We have a tendency to rigidly cling to these stories.

If we can begin to realise that some of the things that we think are simply not true, we can learn not to get so upset when an unpleasant thought enters our head.

I like to think of us all as a web of connections. The way we are feeling is often mirrored by what we see around us.

If we can learn to look at things with awareness, we can feel more present and less anxious about what is happening around us.

Being out in Nature can help us to feel that we are connected to something larger than ourselves. Some people are religious, and some are not but we can all feel a sense of awe when we are out in Nature.

One of the key takeaways that I hope you will receive from reading this book is the importance of us learning to be compassionate to ourselves. This basically means being willing to care for ourselves in the way we would our loved ones.

Kristin Neff is an advocate for self-compassion. In 2011 her book 'Self Compassion: The Proven Power Of Being Kind To Yourself.' was published.

She also offers guided meditations and other activities to support you in your quest to be more compassionate towards yourself.

Tara Brach provides meditations designed to help people to use Mindfulness and compassion to help cope with difficult emotions.

She offers an acronym: RAIN.

This reminds us to

Recognise- this means that we become aware of our emotions.

Allow- this means that we allow them to surface, and we do not attempt to deny or suppress them.

Investigate- means we can explore them further.

Nurture- means that we ensure that we are able to give ourselves the care and attention that we need.

There are many people who have expertise in this area and looking at their work is time well spent.

I mentioned that as we age, we may feel sad about the loss of our youth but with age comes wisdom.

What is wisdom?

To me, wisdom is having experience, knowledge, and good judgement. These can all build in time.

As we get older, we can understand ourselves more and this can enable us to identify how we are feeling and any changes that we might wish to make in our lives.

Once you know what you wish to change you can identify techniques and actions that will help you to bring about the changes you wish to see in your life.

If a particular technique or action doesn't work for you, you can review it and try something else.

This demonstrates that we are getting to know ourselves better and can act in ways that support our wellbeing.

Asking for help and advice when needed is part of being wise.

Sometimes someone you know, and trust is the right person to confide in but sometimes we need professional help.

We may need to consult a doctor and they may refer us for additional support in the form of therapy or counselling.

It can be hard to admit that we need help when we are used to helping others and putting ourselves last, but once we start to prioritise ourselves, we can begin to recognise that sometimes we need help with something rather than struggling alone.

Making a record of how we are feeling can be helpful as we can reflect on this later and see if things are improving. It can be reassuring looking back on a diary entry and noticing that we are feeling better.

It can also be useful reflecting back on how we were feeling at a certain point and comparing it to how we are feeling now. If we are not feeling better, it may be time to review the actions we have been taking, in order to decide if we need to try a new approach.

According to healthline.com It can take 'anywhere from 18 to 254 days for a person to form a new habit and an average of 66 days for a new behaviour to become automatic.'

This means that we need to be willing to stick to something for at least 18 days before we can expect to see many benefits.

I find trying something consistently for a month is doable. If I am struggling after a month, I consider altering my goal or action to see if there is another approach that I might find more helpful.

An example might be carrying out this mindfulness challenge for 30 days and if it doesn't seem to help, you could adapt the sessions in some way to see if that suits you more.

You could swap focusing on your breathing with listening to music to see if that helps.

Forming a new habit is hardest at first. We are not used to it and so we can resist adopting the new behaviour even if we believe that it will help us. If we keep trying, despite not really feeling motivated, we can often find that the habit gets easier to adopt as time goes by.

If we do let things slip it is important not to be too disappointed in ourselves.

Acknowledge that you have come to a halt and resolve to try again.

As American philosopher Elbert Hubbard said, 'There is no failure except in no longer trying.'

I agree with this.

As we age, many of us start to forget people's names or forget to lock our house. People have called this age-related cognitive decline. Our brains change with time as a result of our experiences. This is called neuroplasticity. This means that our brain doesn't have to decline.

A good diet and adopting a healthy lifestyle can slow down cognitive decline. Mindfulness meditation has also been found to help.

Mindfulness meditation is useful in that it can help us with concentration.

In 2014 'Frontiers In Psychology' reviewed the evidence and found that loving-kindness meditation was linked with positive improvements in brain function.

Other studies have suggested that the benefits may not apply to everyone or last for as long as was hoped.

As I have mentioned before, what works well for one person may be less effective for another.

We may benefit from different approaches but if we are able to set aside time each day to focus on our wellbeing that would be great.

Try to observe the present moment without judging it and accept that your mind will wander.

Doing this regularly may greatly benefit you, it is definitely worth trying.

Mindfulness can be adapted to walking and is helpful when trying to sleep. When walking you can move slowly and take in your environment, or you can walk faster and focus on your breath. When you are trying to sleep, lie down somewhere comfortable, close your eyes and mentally scan each part of your body. Which areas feel relaxed and which areas feel tense?

You can relax more deeply by tensing and relaxing each muscle in your body. This can help you to feel calm, relaxed and help you to get ready to drift off to sleep.

In life we have to learn to cope with the many inconveniences, stresses and strains that we encounter.

An example of this might be accidentally locking ourselves out of the house and having to call a locksmith.

It might involve going to the supermarket and realising that we have left our money at home, or it could be us realising that our pet is ill, and we must take them to the vet.

Sometimes something comes along that really upsets our equilibrium such as a family emergency. This can be overwhelming initially but after taking some time to centre yourself and focus on your breath, you are likely to find ways to cope with the situation.

It can help if you are able to recall times when you have coped in a crisis before, and this enables you to feel more capable of dealing with the current situation.

Sometimes a string of traumatic experiences can completely knock us off track. We don't feel we can cope.
This is where friends, family and support services can be a real lifeline.
Being willing to ask for help at this point is part of the solution.

Human beings are remarkably resilient creatures and can cope with an incredible amount of pressure. Being able to remain calm can help us to be clear on our challenges and possible solutions. We are better able to choose appropriate actions to take. Learning how to do this is all part of developing our survival skills.

We are designed to survive but I think we can all agree that we want more than that.

We want to feel fulfilled and purposeful.

We want to connect to other like-minded people and to have a pleasant environment to live in. We wish to be healthy and happy.

Examining who we associate with and what we do to entertain ourselves can enhance our lives. If we discover that we are filling our time doing things that we do not enjoy with people that we go not get on with, we can decide to make some changes.

Assessing the impact of our work and our homelife on how we feel are also useful exercises.

If there is an area that drains us, we can decide upon actions that we can take to improve this situation.

Working on accepting our feelings along with taking good care of our bodies and making sure that we have a healthy diet can all contribute to our wellbeing. Working on our environment and relationships also supports our wellbeing.

The society we live in has an impact on our wellbeing. We may be critical of the political system we live within and wish for change.

Instead of being angry with other people we can begin to find ways that we can make a difference in the world. Positive change is more likely to come about when we are willing to effectively communicate our needs and desires as well as being willing to listen to the needs and desires of others.

I truly believe that the world can become a kinder, fairer place and the way to achieve this is to be clear on our needs and wants as individuals, as well as making the effort to listen to others.

Together we can decide upon the changes that are likely to have the most positive effect for the greatest number of people. This will help us to stop facing and start thriving.

When we are all willing to do what we can to contribute to society, we stand a greater chance of living in a world that works for us all.

We need to be fairer to ourselves as well as others.

We need to consider the impact of our actions on people living now and in future generations.

We won't always get this right, but if our intention is good and we are willing to listen to one another, we will be moving in the right direction.

People make mistakes which may affect their judgement but if they are willing to correct their mistakes and we are willing to correct ours, we will be able to forgive one another and more forward together.

We have almost come to the end of this book.

Let's spend some time summarising what we have been thinking about.

The 30-Day Challenge Summary:

Start by rating your mood out of 10.

Next, rate the key areas of your life out of 10 to help you see where things are good and where change might be needed.

Try Mindfulness for 10 minutes a day for 30 days and make a note of any observations or discoveries.

Do something for yourself each day. This can be a small thing like taking time to listen to a piece of music that you enjoy or having a bubble bath. It doesn't matter what it is as long as it is something you enjoy. Committing to doing something nice for yourself daily is important and you deserve it.

At the end of the 30 days, you can see what has helped and make sure you find time to do more of it in the future.

30 Suggestions:

Here are some suggestions for things you can do for yourself. You can choose any of these or think of some ideas of your own that would really appeal to you. I would love to hear about any activities that you found particularly enjoyable.

1. Go out in Nature. It might be that you choose to spend time in your garden if you have one. You could visit a wood, park, or beach. The possibilities are endless. If you can't go outside, look out of a window and notice what is happening in the sky. There may be interesting clouds or birds flying around.
2. Julia Cameron wrote a book called 'The Artist's Way' where she suggested you take yourself out on an 'artist's date.' You don't need to be an artist to do this. She is talking about you visiting somewhere that you find interesting and rejuvenating. You might choose to go to the cinema or to a wildlife park, for example.
3. Make yourself a gift. You could bake yourself a cake, for example.

4. Watch a favourite film.
5. Listen to your favourite music.
6. Have a lovely shower or bubble bath. You could light some candles.
7. Cook your favourite meal.
8. Watch a comedy and have a really good laugh!
9. Buy yourself a card and write a lovely message for yourself in it.
10. Do your favourite exercise. You might like swimming or cycling, for example.
11. Read an interesting book.
12. Eat your favourite snack.
13. Drink your favourite drink.
14. Wear your favourite clothes.
15. Learn a new skill. You might choose to learn some phrases of a new language for example.
16. Take a photo of something that makes you smile.
17. Go somewhere you have never been to before.

18. Order your favourite takeaway meal.
19. Arrange to meet a friend.
20. Go to the beach and find a beautiful stone or shell.
21. Visit a museum or gallery.
22. Sing!
23. Do some drawing or painting.
24. Do some writing.
25. Look at some old photographs.
26. Spend some time on your own.
27. Eat your favourite fruit.
28. Fly a kite.
29. Do a jigsaw or play a board game.
30. Buy a new plant.

How is your Mindfulness experiment going?

I have found mine to be an interesting and valuable experience.

I have created a newsletter on 'Substack' where I have been noting down anything that I have noticed. Doing this has helped to keep me on track. I have noticed how easily distracted I can be, how thoughts can enter my head and stop me focusing on my breath. I have noted my successes too such as the time when I was able to focus on my senses rather than my thoughts and feelings which helped me to stay in the moment.

If you would be interested in looking at my Substack newsletter, here is a link to one of the pages:

https://cathyshuter.substack.com/p/mindfulness-day-27?r=1y43l&s=w&utm_campaign=post&utm_medium=web

I have been productive during the time I have been mindfully meditating. I have added to this book each day, spent time tidying my environment and improving my fitness.

I have definitely noticed that I been less concerned or preoccupied by events featured on The News. I realise there are things I can control and things that I can't. Understanding this has helped me a lot.

I feel generally calmer, and I have coped when I have had car trouble and trouble with my heating system in the same week. Sometimes events like this can have a negative impact on me but this month has seen me more accepting of whatever comes along, and this has enabled me to enjoy myself more.

Another benefit has been that I have been less distracted by the 'next shiny object' to come along and push me off course.

What do I mean by this?

Well, I am fascinated by Personal Development, writing and creating. I have attended a lot of free webinars on these subjects, over the years. Every time I am offered a new book or course, I have a tendency to leap in and buy it if it is within my budget.

A lot of my purchases have been very interesting and have provided me with inspiration for my own work, but I realise that if I have a clear idea of what I wish to achieve next in my life, I need to be more discerning.

This week I attended an exciting webinar about writing and publishing. The content was excellent. I was able to gain a lot from what I was being offered without feeling the need to make any additional purchases. What was being offered would be extremely useful to many people attending and I think the package being sold would be helpful to me in a year or two if my writing and publishing progresses at the pace, I anticipate it will.

Before my Mindfulness experiment, I suspect I would have gone ahead and purchased the package before I was ready.

How does Mindfulness help with this?

I think it helps me to be more focused on my needs and less distracted by impulses.

After the experiment is over, I have decided that I will continue with my Mindfulness sessions, Aand I will also continue using my Substack newsletter as it is a good way to stay in touch with people.

Congratulations!

You have come to the end of the book. I hope you have enjoyed reading it and carrying out the activities within it.

I would love to hear from you. Feel free to email me: cathee@hotmail.co.uk to let me know how things are going.

I think the key message here is:

It is important to start by focusing on yourself. Make time for yourself every day and ask yourself:

What do I need to help me on my way?

Making sure you look after yourself properly will stop you from fading.

Printed in Great Britain
by Amazon

86939516R10078